FANTASTIC BEASTS

AND WHERE TO FIND THEM™

COLOURING
AND
CREATIVITY BOOK

Scholastic Ltd.

An Insight Editions Book

Fantastic Beasts and Where to Find Them™ is the story of
Newt Scamander and the magical creatures he finds and rescues.

Newt Scamander is the world's most famous – and only – Magizoologist.
That means that he studies magical creatures.

Newt keeps all of the fantastic beasts he finds
in his magical leather case.

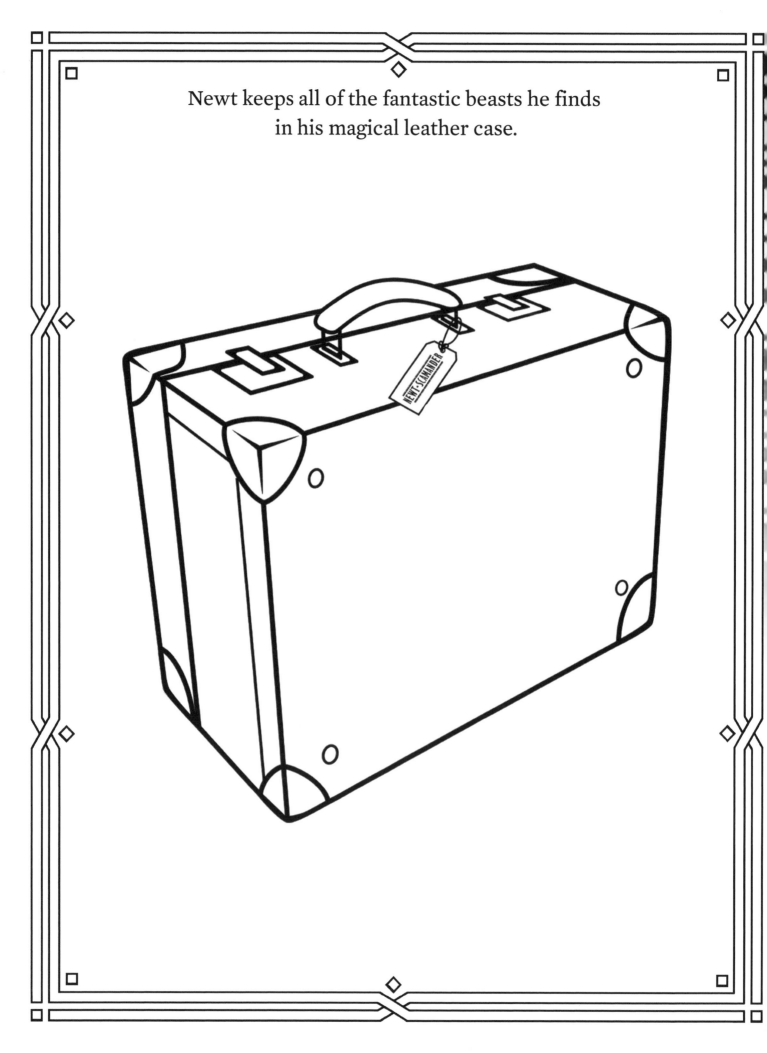

When Newt doesn't want people to discover the creatures
in his case, he sets the lock to "MUGGLE WORTHY".

Newt's magical case holds all of his supplies.
If you were going on a trip to search for fantastic beasts,
what would you take with you?

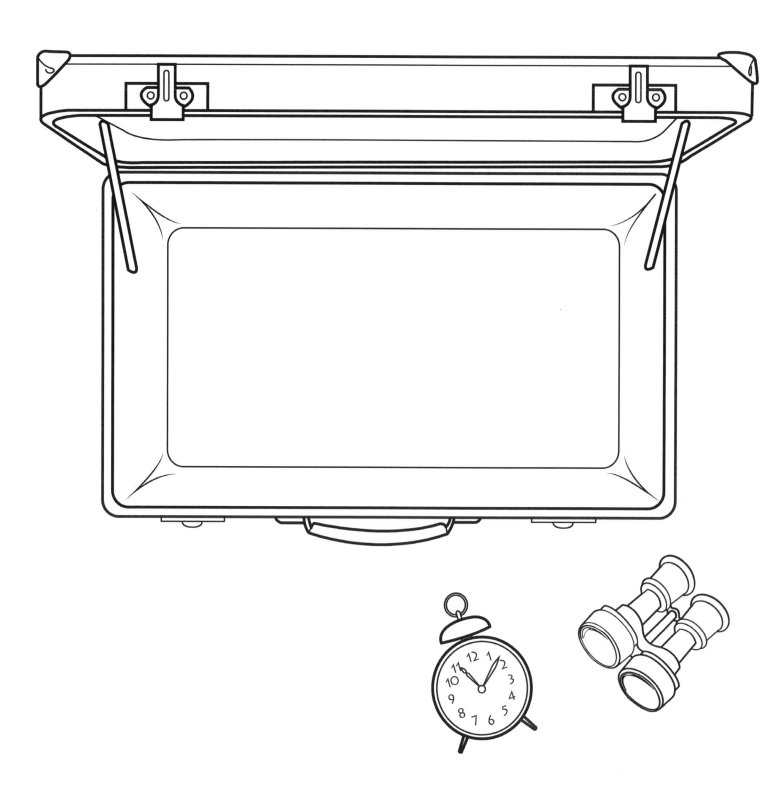

Newt has a special insignia using his initials that
identifies many of his personal belongings.
Create your own insignia below using your initials.

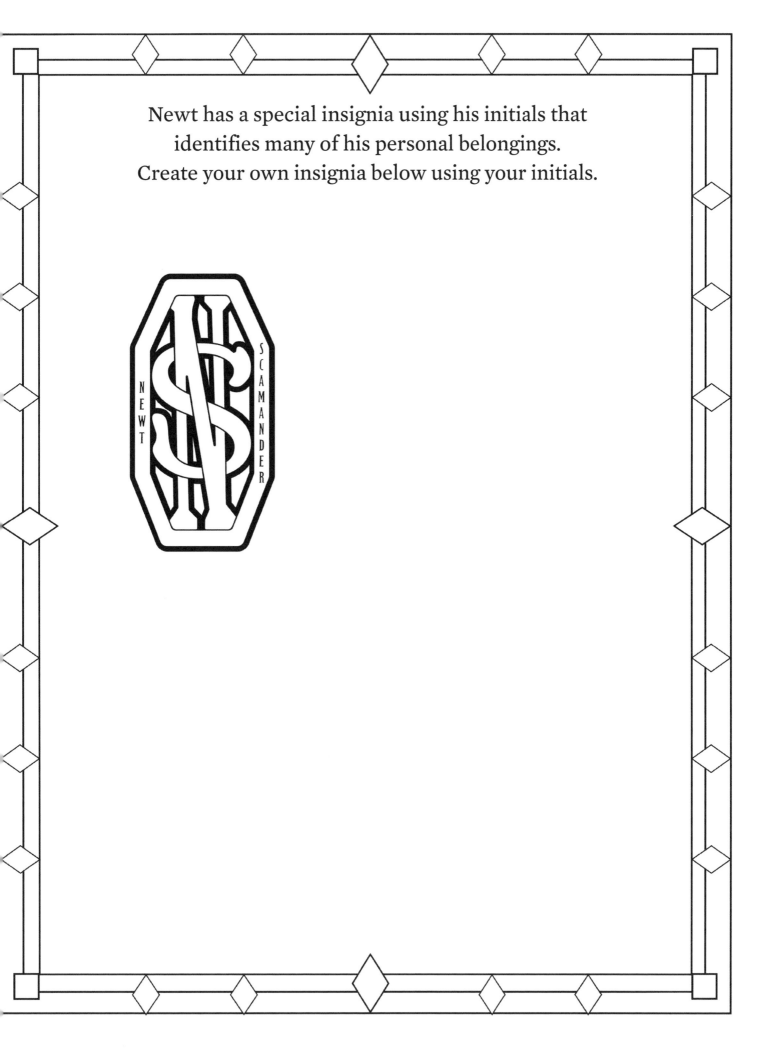

Newt keeps all his notes about the creatures he finds in his Magizoologist diary. Decorate and colour your own diary.

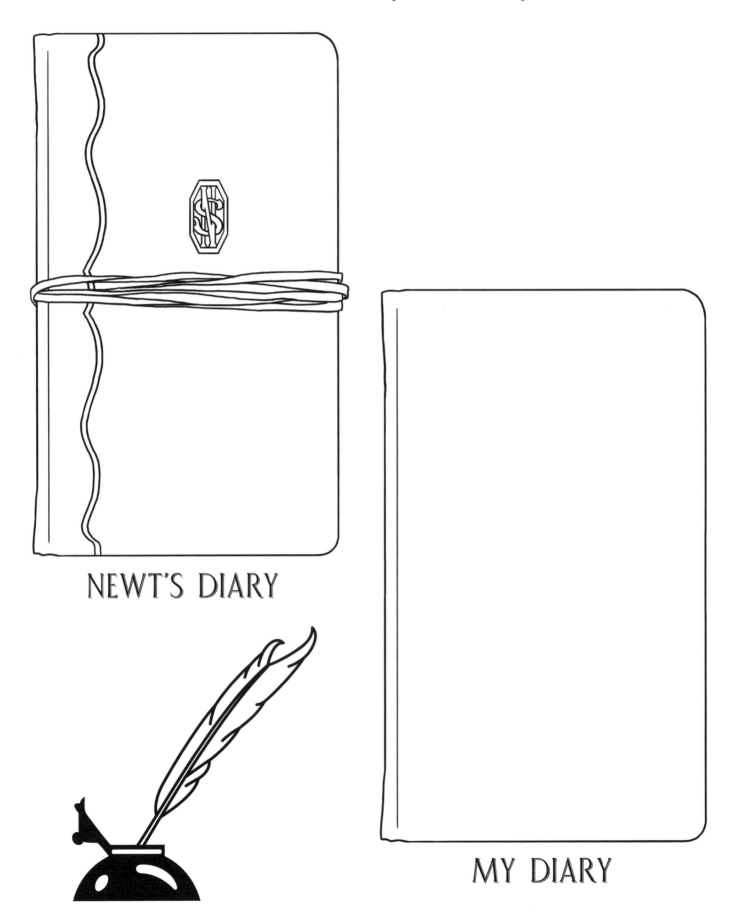

NEWT'S DIARY

MY DIARY

Newt studies everything around
him and takes lots of careful notes.
Practise your own observation skills by noticing
what's around you right now.

OBSERVATIONS

Where are you?

_____
_____
_____
_____

Who or what can you see?

_____
_____
_____
_____
_____

What sounds can you hear?

_____
_____
_____
_____

What can you smell?

_____
_____
_____
_____

Where would you hide if you were a magical beast?

_____
_____
_____
_____

One of the creatures that Newt has in his case is a Niffler.
This cute beast looks a bit like a platypus.

The Niffler is attracted to sparkly and shiny objects.

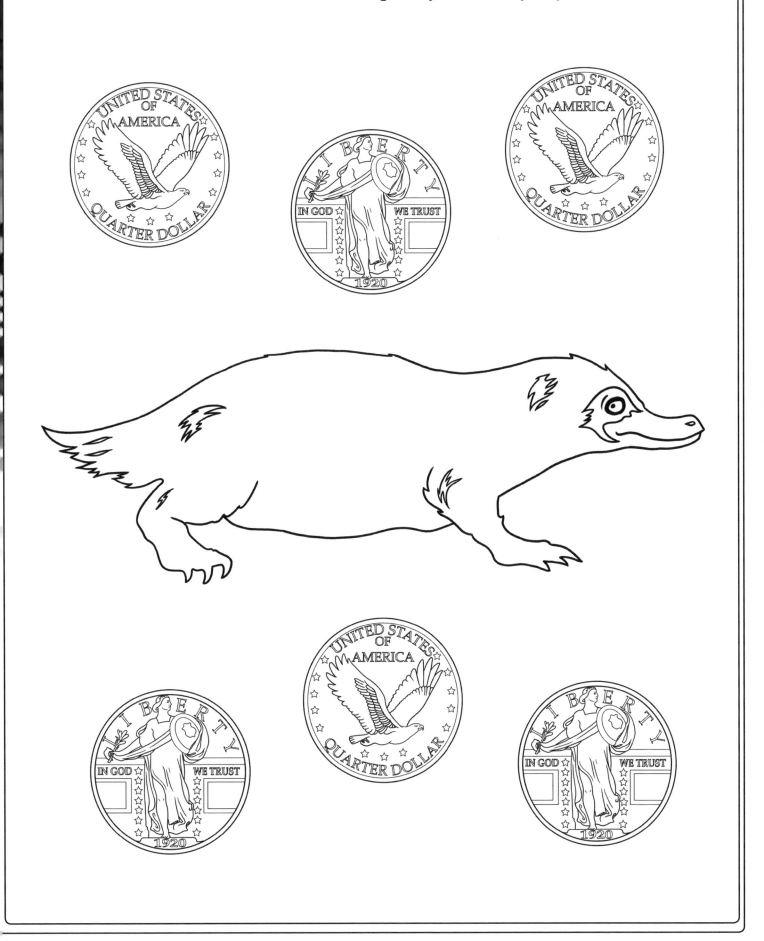

Another of Newt's creatures is the Swooping Evil.
It is a large butterfly-like creature that emerges from a small cocoon.

Colour the cocoon and draw a flying creature below.

A Bowtruckle is a useful beast to have around, especially in case a lock needs picking.

Nothing That Occurs in Nature Can Be Unnatural

Some of the creatures that Newt cares for hatch from eggs, like the Occamy. Draw what kind of magical creatures you think hatched from the eggs below!

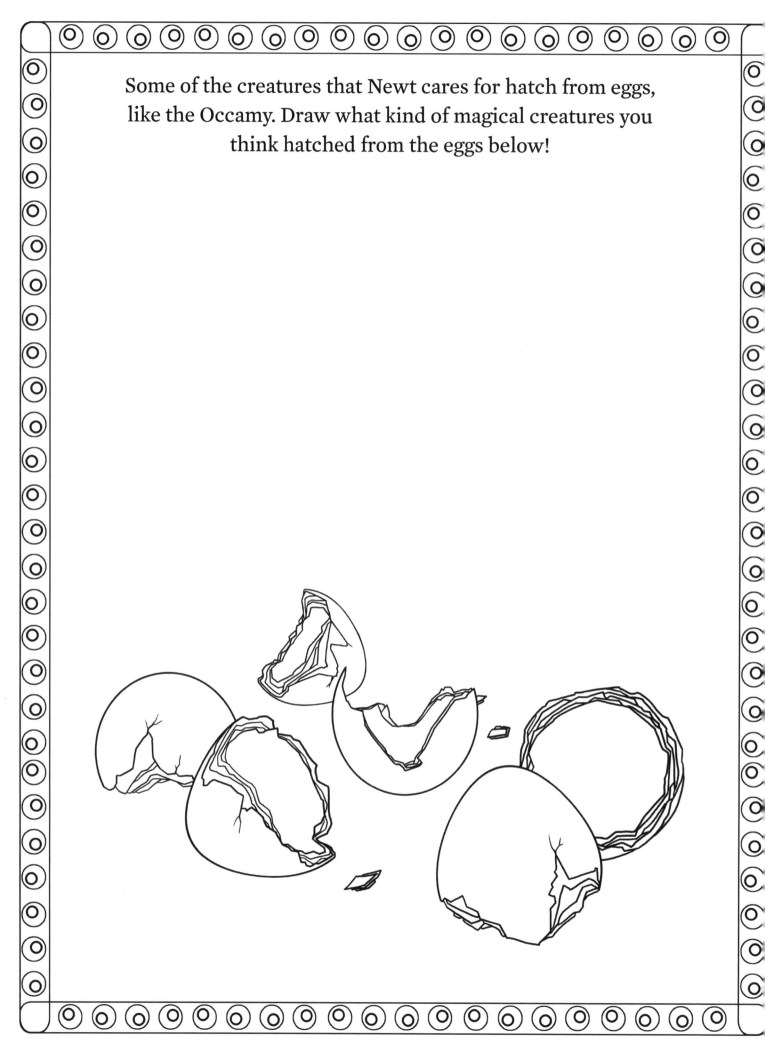

The Occamy can grow or shrink to fit the space it is in.
Newt and Tina use a teapot – and a clever trick –
to catch the missing Occamy!

The Runespoor is a three-headed snake.
The heads often bicker in disagreement and start fighting.

MACUSA is the Magical Congress of the United States of America.
It is located in the Woolworth Building in New York City.

PORPENTINA GOLDSTEIN

Tina Goldstein works for MACUSA in the Wand Permit Office.

Like all witches and wizards, Newt and the people
who work at MACUSA have their own wands.

Newt Scamander

Tina Goldstein

Queenie Goldstein

Executioner

Each wand is as different as the witch or wizard it chooses.

AUROR

SERAPHINA PICQUERY

PERCIVAL GRAVES

What kind of wand would you like to have? Draw it below.

MACUSA takes privacy and security very seriously!

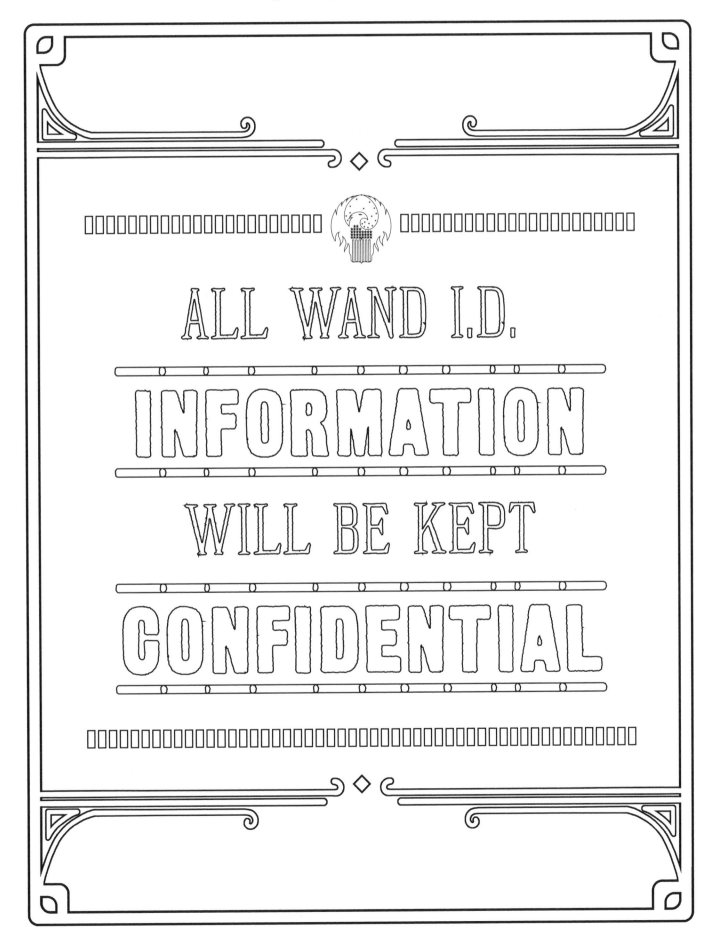

ALL WAND I.D.

INFORMATION

WILL BE KEPT

CONFIDENTIAL

Non-magical people are known to the
American wizarding community as No-Majs.

No-Majs!

No-Magics

Non-Wizards

Jacob Kowalski is a No-Maj who meets Newt
when they are both at Steen National Bank.

Oh, no! Newt accidentally switches cases with Jacob.
Decorate the two cases so they are easy to tell apart.

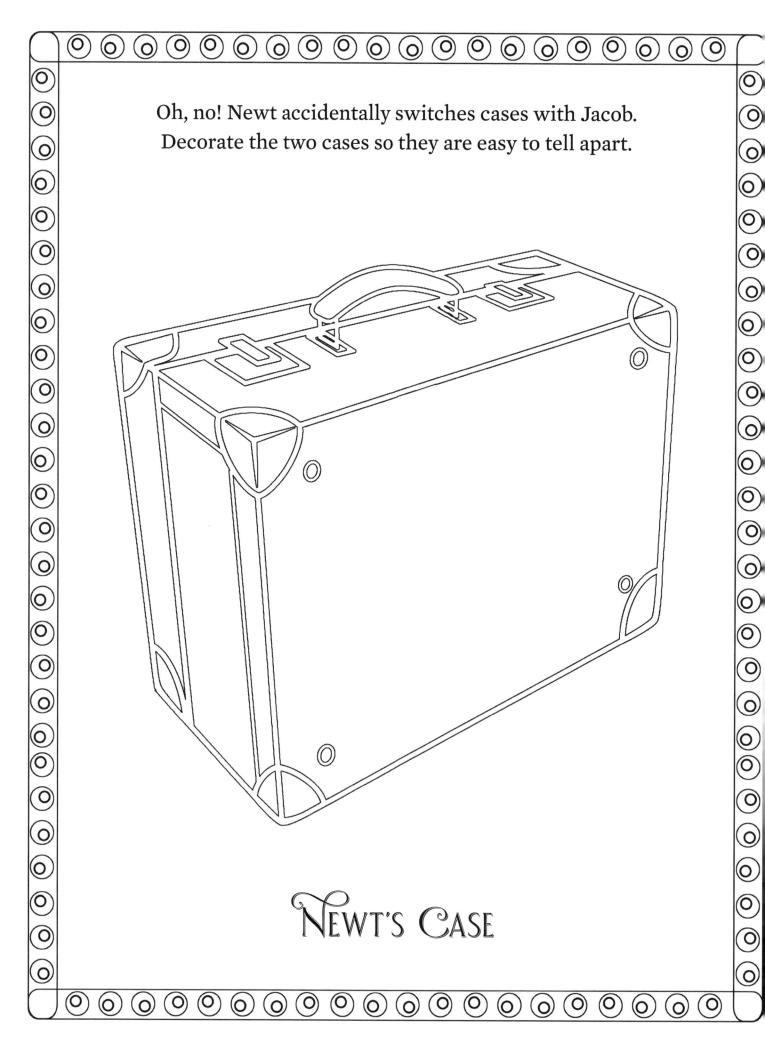

NEWT'S CASE

Newt's case contains all his creatures,
while Jacob's contains delicious pastries.

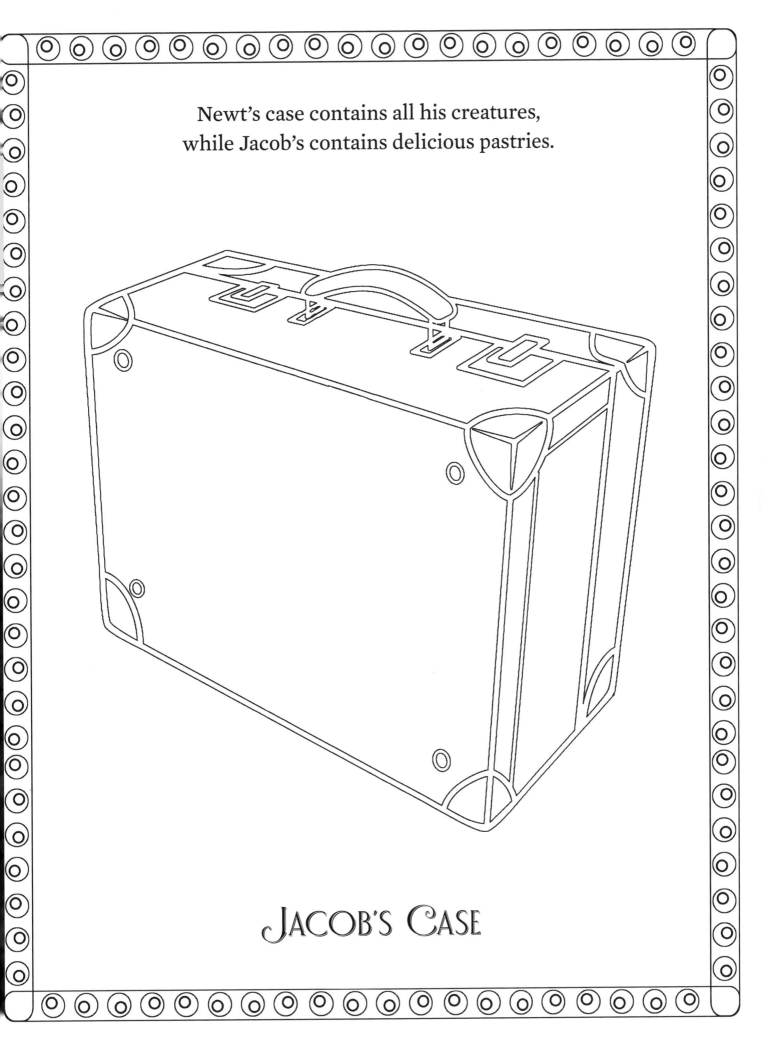

JACOB'S CASE

Jacob Kowalski needs a loan from the bank to open his own bakery.

Jacob wants to open a bakery and make his own pastries.
Help get him started by drawing some cakes below!

There are lots of shops near Jacob's apartment.
Create your own signs in the scene below.

FANTASTIC BEASTS
AND WHERE TO FIND THEM
PORPENTINA GOLDSTEIN
TM & © WBEI (s16)

PERCIVAL GRAVES
FANTASTIC BEASTS
AND WHERE TO FIND THEM
TM & © WBEI (s16)

FANTASTIC BEASTS
AND WHERE TO FIND THEM
QUEENIE GOLDSTEIN
LEGILIMENCY
TM & © WBEI (s16)

JACOB KOWALSKI
FANTASTIC BEASTS
AND WHERE TO FIND THEM
KOWALSKI
TM & © WBEI (s16)

NEWT SCAMANDER
MAGIZOOLOGIST
TM & © WBEI (s16)

Nothing That Occurs in Nature Can Be Unnatural
FANTASTIC BEASTS
TM & © WBEI (s16)

HOOF HEALER OINTMENT
TM & © WBEI (s16)

BEAK BALM
TM & © WBEI (s16)

TM & © WBEI (s16)

STUPEFY
TM & © WBEI (s16)

No-Majs!
No-Magics
non-Wizards
TM & © WBEI (s16)

TM & © WBEI (s16)

MUGGLE WORTHY
TM & © WBEI (s16)

TM & © WBEI (s16)

MUGGLE = NO-MAJ
TM & © WBEI (s16)

WANDED AND EXTREMELY DANGEROUS
BEASTS
TM & © WBEI (s16)

NEWT SCAMANDER
TM & © WBEI (s16)

OBLIVIATE
TM & © WBEI (s16)

TM & © WBEI (s16)

TM & © WBEI (s16)

BECOME AN OBLIVIATOR!
RECRUITING NOW
EVERY HALF MOON
OF THE MONTH

PO# Here

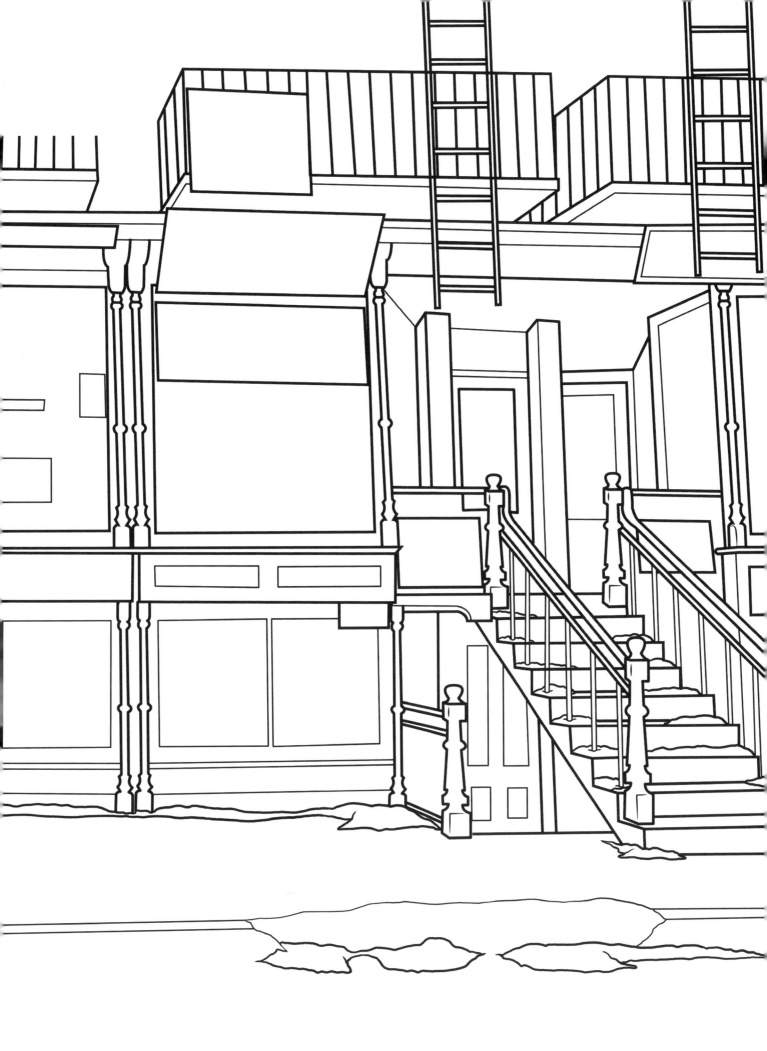

Oh, no! An Erumpent, a massive creature that resembles a rhinoceros, escapes from Newt's case and ends up destroying Jacob's apartment.

Draw what happened below.

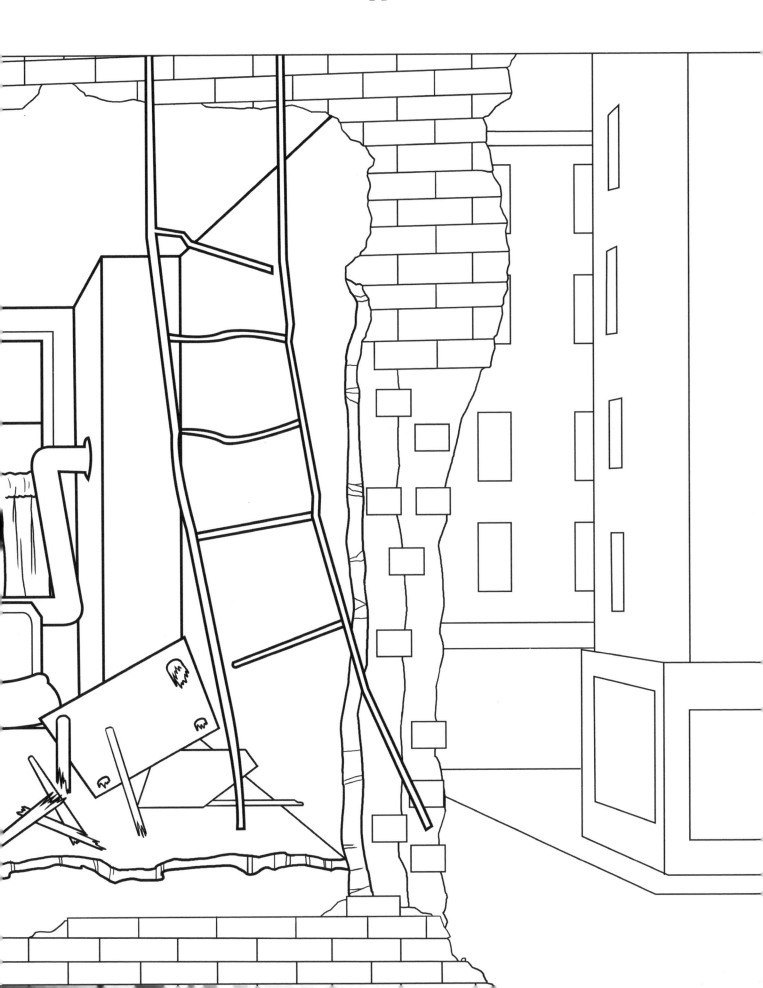

It's important that Newt finds the Erumpent quickly!

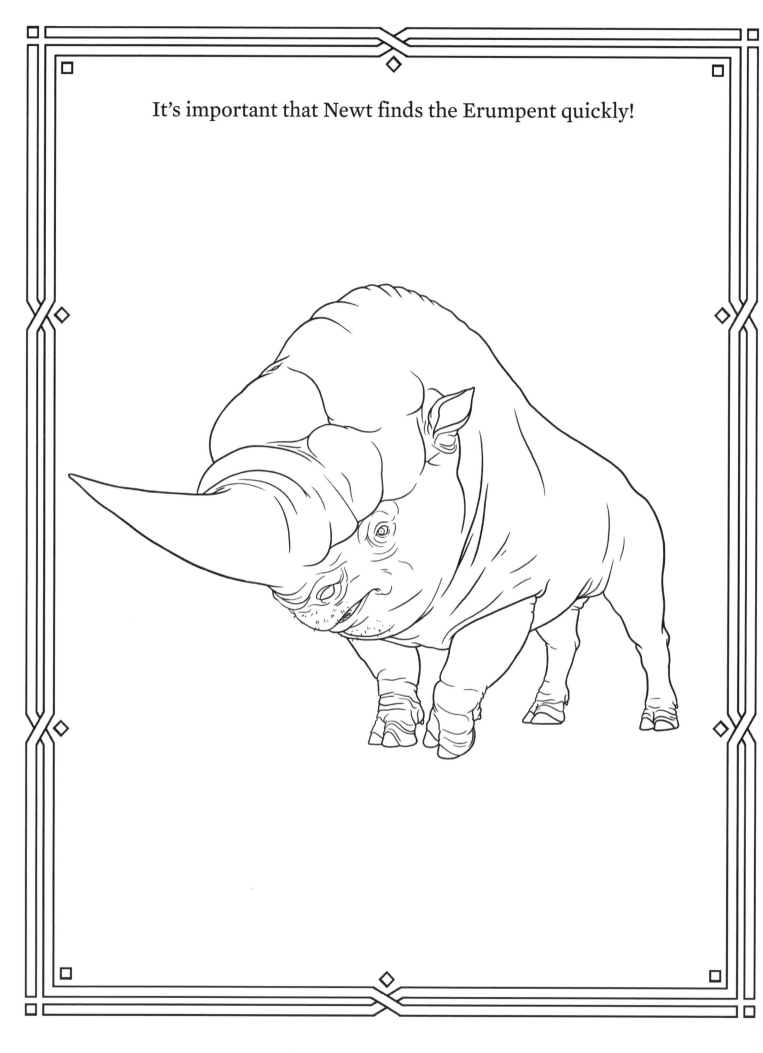

Newt uses this musk to make himself smell appealing to the escaped Erumpent. Hopefully, once the Erumpent gets a whiff of the musk, Newt can lure her back inside the case.

APOTHECARIUM LIMUS
— London —

ERUMPENT
MUSK

№

24

RECOMMENDED DOSE: ¾℥

MACUSA hosts conferences for witches and wizards from all over the world.

Tina uses an ID to gain entry into her job at MACUSA.
Create your own ID below so you can be official, too.

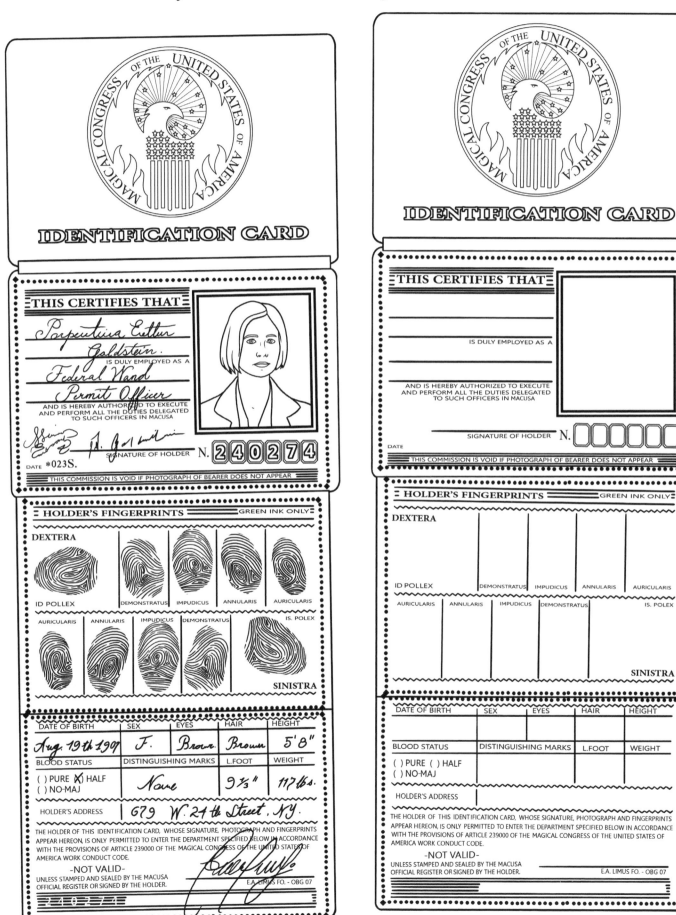

There is a Magical Exposure Threat Level Clock hanging in the MACUSA lobby. This dial alerts witches and wizards to strange magical happenings in the world.

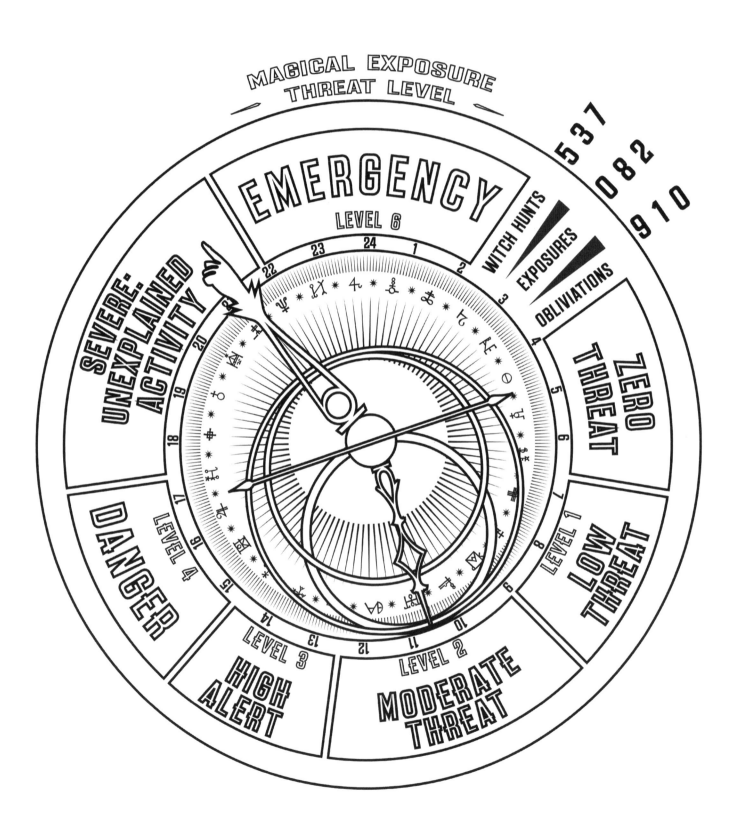

Create your own Magical Exposure Threat Level Clock below.

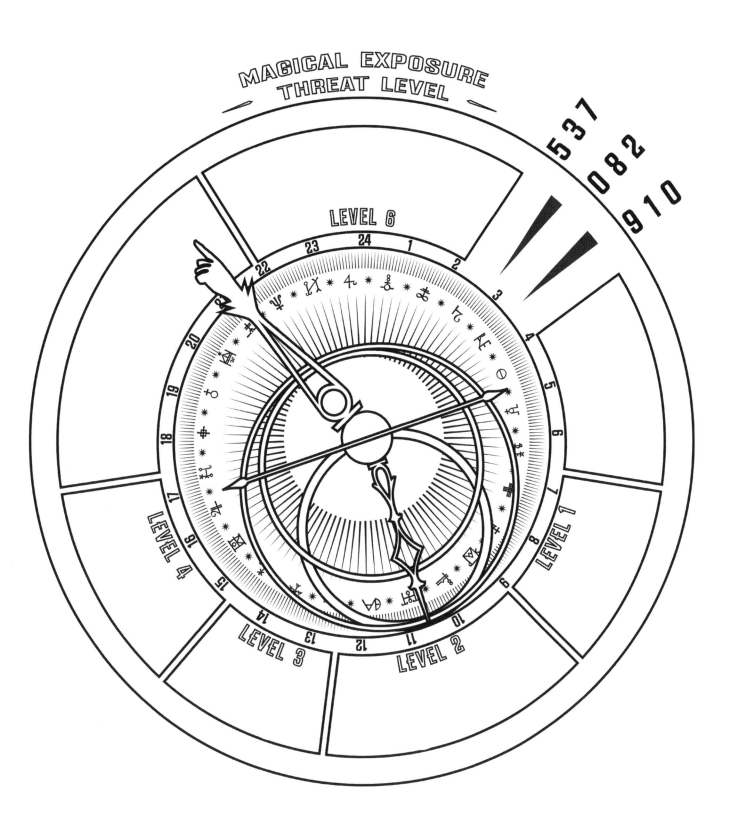

MACUSA has a Real-Time Hex Indicator of the United States.

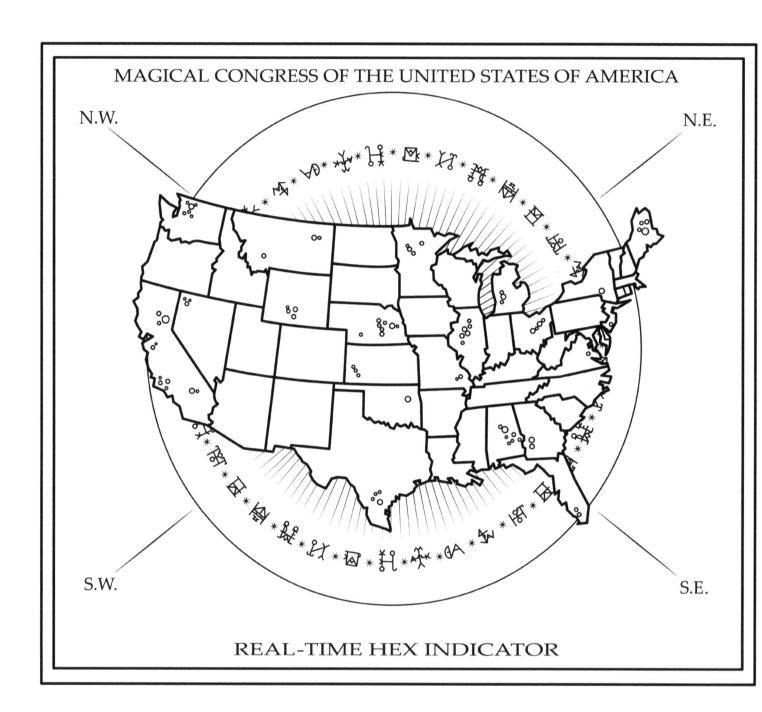

N.W.

N.E.

MAGICAL CONGRESS OF THE UNITED STATES OF AMERICA

S.W.

S.E.

REAL-TIME HEX INDICATOR

Seraphina Picquery is a powerful witch and the President of MACUSA.

Percival Graves is the Director of Magical Security at MACUSA.
He is one of Seraphina's most trusted advisors.

New York City is the home of many witches and wizards.

MACUSA has lots of signs with instructions for their employees.

YOU CURSE IT, YOU CURE IT!

Only witches and wizards are allowed to work at MACUSA.

Extra, extra! Something strange is going on in the wizarding world. Draw a picture and write a headline that tells the story!

Queenie Goldstein is a fun-loving witch with an excellent sense of style.

Queenie is a Legilimens, which means
she knows what other people are thinking.

If you were a Legilimens, how would you use your powers?

At home, I'd read _____'s mind so I could find out:

_____

_____

_____

At school, I'd read _____'s mind so I could find out:

_____

_____

_____

On the playground, I'd read _____'s mind so I could find out:

_____

_____

_____

During a wizarding duel, I'd read _____'s mind so I could find out:

_____

_____

_____

The American Charmer is a fashion magazine for witches.

The AMERICAN *Charmer*

AUGUST 1926

SPELLBINDING SUMMER SIZZLERS!
Latest cuts straight from the catwalk

Queenie loves to know all about current style trends.

Tina and Queenie live together in an apartment in New York City.

In addition to being sisters,
Tina and Queenie are
also best friends.

Newt and his friends use spells to help on their adventures. *Accio* is a summoning spell, and *Obliviate* is a memory-erasing spell.

Create your own spell name and write it below.

The purpose of this spell is: _____

_____

_____

Henry Shaw is a candidate who is looking to get re-elected.
Senator Shaw and his father do not believe in witches and wizards.

If you wanted to run for political office,
what would your campaign poster look like?

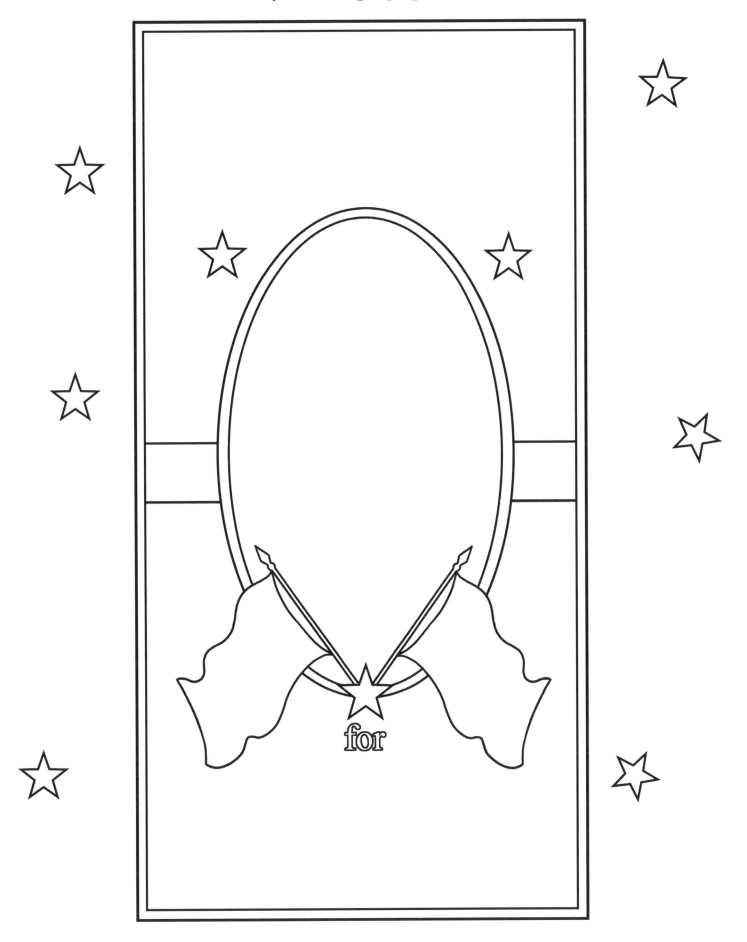

for

Newt has a shed where he keeps everything
he needs to care for his creatures.
Draw a shed where you would keep all your favourite things.

Newt has lots of special plants growing in his shed.
Draw your own plants in the pots below. Are any of them magical?

Newt's shed is full of all kinds of scientific charts
and boards for tracking beast behaviour.

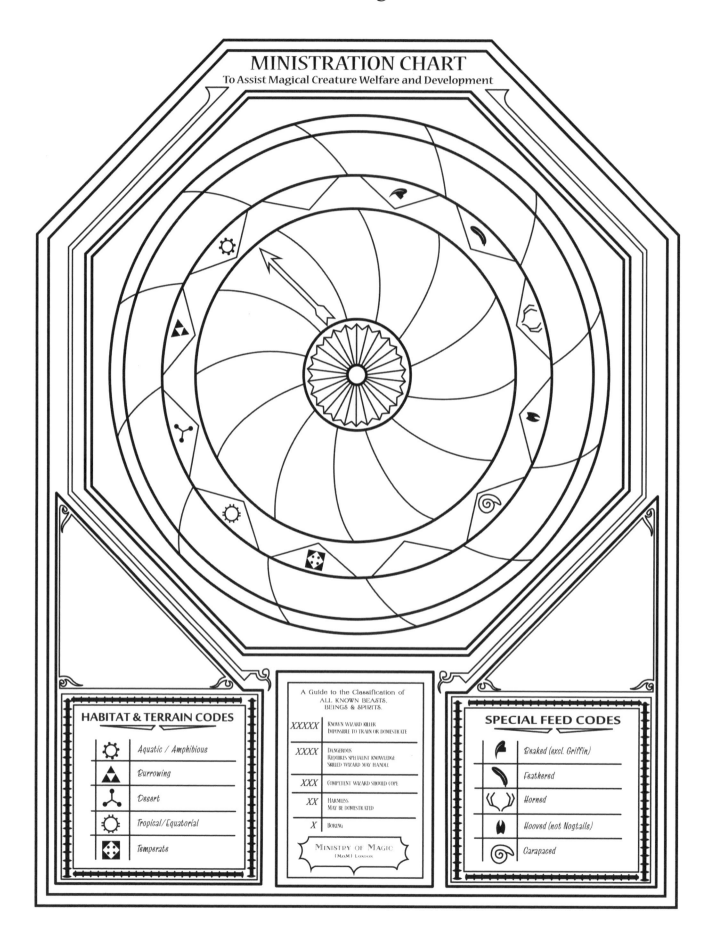

MINISTRATION CHART
To Assist Magical Creature Welfare and Development

HABITAT & TERRAIN CODES

⚙	Aquatic / Amphibious
▲▲	Burrowing
⅄	Desert
☼	Tropical/Equatorial
◈	Temperate

A Guide to the Classification of
ALL KNOWN BEASTS,
BEINGS & SPIRITS.

XXXXX	KNOWN WIZARD KILLER IMPOSSIBLE TO TRAIN OR DOMESTICATE
XXXX	DANGEROUS REQUIRES SPECIALIST KNOWLEDGE SKILLED WIZARD MAY HANDLE
XXX	COMPETENT WIZARD SHOULD COPE
XX	HARMLESS MAY BE DOMESTICATED
X	BORING

MINISTRY OF MAGIC
(MoM) LONDON

SPECIAL FEED CODES

◗	Beaked (excl. Griffin)
⟩	Feathered
⟨⟩	Horned
◖	Hooved (not Nogtails)
◉	Carapaced

Newt has beakers and vials full of special solutions
he needs to care for his creatures.

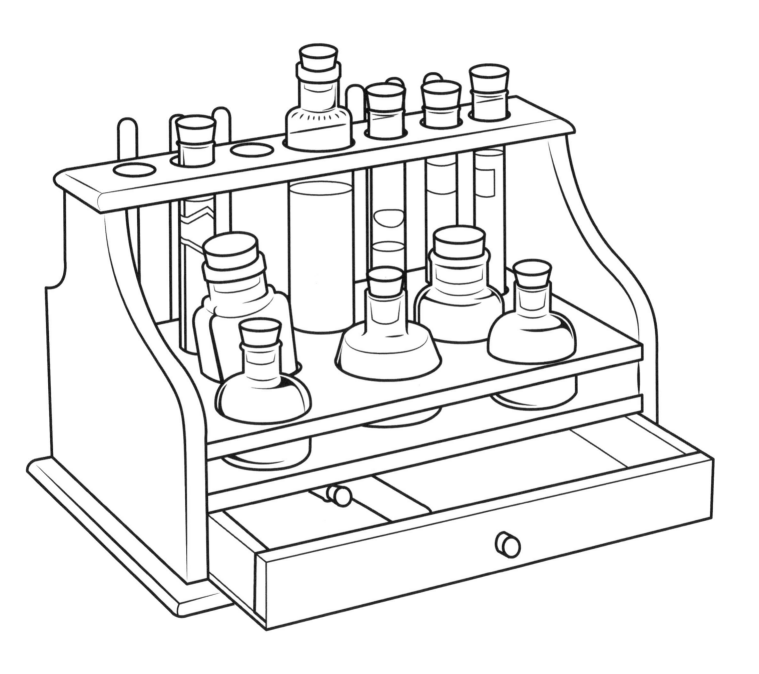

Newt uses reference books like this one in his study of magical creatures. Decorate the book below.

In his shed, Newt displays artefacts from his travels.

What kind of beast do you think Newt will see
in the magnifying glass below? Draw it here.

Glass jars come in handy for storing Newt's potions in his shed.

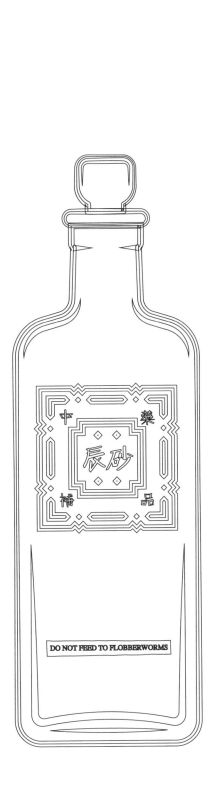

THE OWL AIRFORCE

TRUE LIFE TALES OF WAR IN EUROPE

Newt uses a typewriter to type notes for a book he is writing.
Write down some of your own observations about
a magical beast that you've found!

OBSERVATIONS:

Nights out in New York City can be very glamorous.
Draw special necklaces that Queenie and Tina could wear.

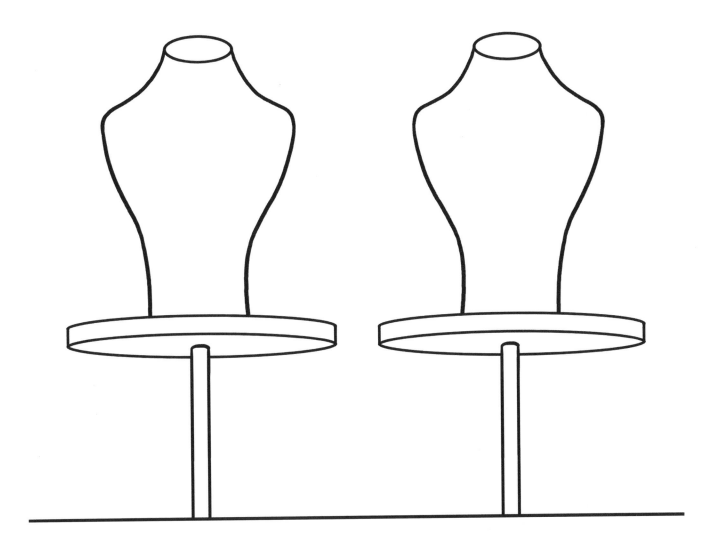

The Blind Pig is a nightclub in New York
where witches and wizards gather.

THE
BLIND PIG

Enchanting. Beguiling. Alluring.

The Blind Pig has shelves and shelves full of
interesting and mysterious bottles.

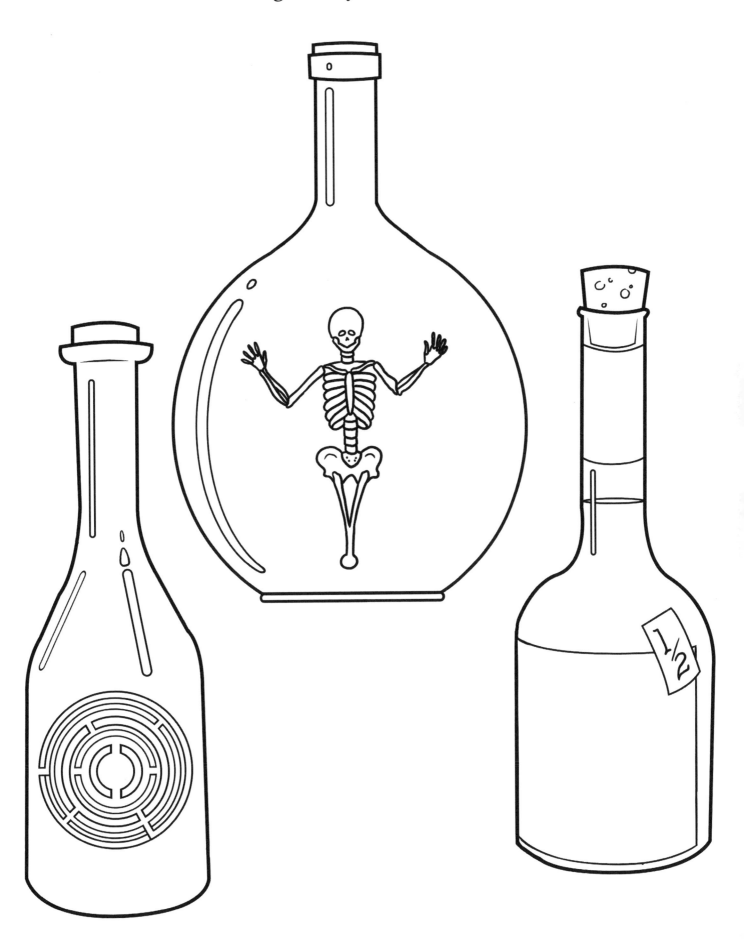

Some of the witches and wizards at The Blind Pig are wanted criminals!
Design your own wanted poster below.

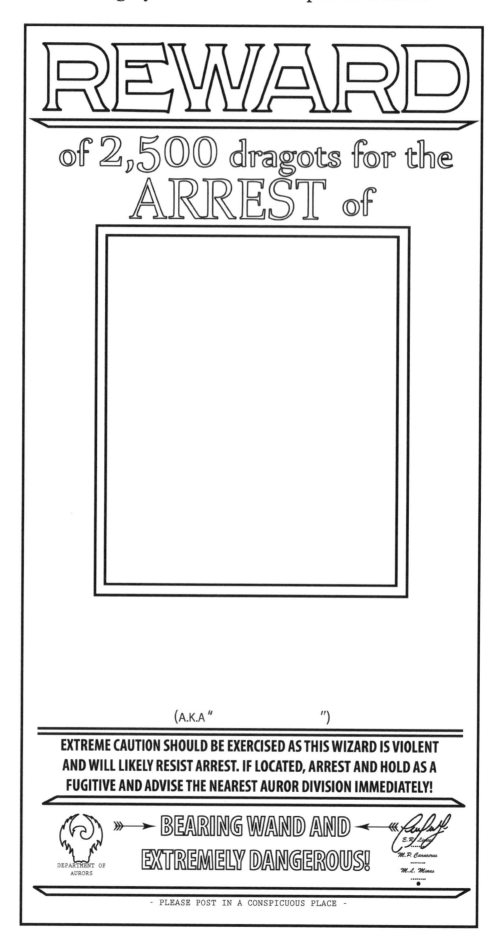

Newt has an exciting time in New York City! On the postcard below, write to a friend about what you would do if you were in the "Big Apple".

www.fantasticbeasts.co.uk

Scholastic Children's Books
Euston House, 24 Eversholt Street,
London NW1 1DB, UK

A division of Scholastic Ltd
London ~ New York ~ Toronto ~ Sydney ~ Auckland
Mexico City ~ New Delhi ~ Hong Kong

First published in the US by Scholastic Inc, 2016
Published in the UK by Scholastic Ltd, 2016

ISBN 978 1407 17343 6

Printed and bound in Germany

2 4 6 8 10 9 7 5 3 1

Produced by Insight Editions

I N S I G H T EDITIONS

PO Box 3088
San Rafael, CA 94912
www.insighteditions.com

Publisher: Raoul Goff
Art Director: Chrissy Kwasnik
Executive Editor: Vanessa Lopez
Project Editor: Greg Solano
Production Editor: Rachel Anderson
Illustrations by Francesca Harvie

www.scholastic.co.uk